Cover Image Credit/Copyright Attribution: IIIerlok_Xolms/Shutterstock

John Mowitt holds the Leadership Chair in the Critical Humanities at the University of Leeds. His publications range widely over the fields of culture, politics and theory. His most recent book, *Sounds: The Ambient Humanities*, was published by University of California Press in 2015. He is a senior co-editor of *Cultural Critique*.

Tracks from the Crypt

John Mowitt

**Bibliographical Information of the
German National Library**
The German National Library lists this publication in the
Deutsche Nationalbibliografie (German National Biblio-
graphy); detailed bibliographic information is available
online at http://dnb.d-nb.de.

Contents

Configurations of Film: Series Foreword

Scalable across a variety of formats and standardized in view of global circulation, the moving image has always been both an image of movement and an image on the move. Over the last three decades, digital production technologies, communication networks and distribution platforms have taken the scalability and mobility of film to a new level. Beyond the classical *dispositif* of the cinema, new forms and knowledges of cinema and film have emerged, challenging the established approaches to the study of film. The conceptual framework of index, *dispositif* and canon, which defined cinema as photochemical image technology with a privileged bond to reality, a site of public projection, and a set of works from auteurs from specific national origins, can no longer account for the current multitude of moving images and the trajectories of their global movements. The term "post-cinema condition," which was first proposed by film theorists more than a decade ago to describe the new cultural and technological order of moving images, retained an almost melancholic attachment to that which the cinema no longer was. Moving beyond such attachments, the concept of "configurations of film" aims to account for moving images in terms of their operations, forms and formats, locations and infrastructures, expanding the field of cinematic knowledges beyond the arts and the aesthetic, while retaining a focus on film as privileged site for the production of cultural meaning, for social action and for political conflict.

The series "Configurations of Film" presents pointed interventions in this field of debate by emerging and established international scholars associated with the DFG-funded Graduate Research Training Program (Graduiertenkolleg) "Konfigurationen des Films" at Goethe University Frankfurt. The contributions to the series aim to explore and expand our understanding of configurations of film in both a contemporary and historical perspective, combining film and media theory with media history to address key problems in the development of new analytical frameworks for the moving image on the move.

*On devrait commencer à savoir que ce ne
sont pas les gens qui communiquent …, mais
les objets (énoncés, images) qui se communiquent. [We should know by now that it
is not people who communicate, but rather
objects (statements, images) that communicate
by themselves.]*
Serge Daney, "La remise en scène" (1976)[1]

Introduction

Rebecca Boguska, Vinzenz Hediger

Is film a medium of communication?

This is a basic question of film studies. It is about as old as
the field itself, and the discursive frameworks and underlying
assumptions that make the question relevant are about as old
as the medium, or the art form, of cinema itself. As John Durham
Peters argues, "only since the late nineteenth century have we
defined ourselves in terms our ability to *communicate* with one
another," to the point where "'[c]ommunication' is one of the
characteristic concepts of the twentieth century" (1999, 1).

For most of the twentieth century up until the 1970s, the question
of whether film was a medium of communication seemed to have
been settled in the affirmative. During the Second World War,
Princeton psychologists Carl Hovland, Arthur Lumsdaine, and
Fred Sheffield studied the effects of the US Army's "Why we fight"
films, which Frank Capra produced, on the motivations and political persuasions of US soldiers. As a matter of course, the three
researchers assumed that film, like radio or the newspaper, was

1   For the pointer, we thank Pierre Eugène.

a form of mass communication. When they published the study as a book in 1949, Princeton University Press chose *Experiments on Mass Communication* as the title. "Film" does not even appear in the subtitle. With almost continuous reprints since its first publication, it remains one of the founding texts of empirical media research. Incidentally, the study showed that soldiers learned a lot about the reasons and historical contexts of the war, but emerged from contact with the films with their belief structures and political convictions largely unaffected. What Hovland, Lumsdaine, and Sheffield found was—at least in part—a failure of film to communicate (2017).

One could argue, of course, that this partial failure underscores film's standing as a modern, twentieth-century medium and art form. Citing the films of Bergman, Antonioni, and Tarkovsky, and "scenes of stammering face-to-face relations" alongside the dramatic works of Beckett, Sartre, and Ionesco, Peters reminds us that "much twentieth-century drama, art, cinema, and literature examines the impossibility of communication between people" (Peteres 1999, 2). And the preoccupation with the absence of communication extends beyond the arts into the social sciences and social theory. Probably more in the same modernist spirit than is generally acknowledged, Niklas Luhmann's theory of social systems is predicated on the improbability, rather than the inevitability of communication (1995).

In the late 1960s and early 1970s, when film studies emerged as an academic field, Christian Metz addressed the question of film as a medium of communication along similar lines. For Metz, film was not quite a medium of communication, or rather, it was more than that. Writing as a linguist turned film theorist, Metz shifted the framework from communication research to semiotics and argued:

> A cinema is not a system, but contains several of them. It seems not to have signs, but this is because its own are very different from those of spoken language; in addition, the

> domain of signification largely goes beyond that of signs …. It goes beyond that of communication strictly speaking: the cinema, it is true, does not authorize the immediate play of bilateral exchange, but it is not the only semiotic system to behave in this way; nothing directly responds to a myth, to a folktale, to a ritual, to a culinary or clothing system, to a piece of music. (Metz 1974, 288)

Cinema, in other words, is more a resource of cultural meanings than a medium of communication, if indeed by communication we understand primarily face-to-face communication, the "immediate play of bilateral exchange" of which Metz speaks here.

For cinema studies as a field of research, Metz's shift, from a communications to a semiotics framework and from "bilateral exchange" to cinema as a resource of meaning embedded in social practice, is a paradigmatic gesture. It secures a surplus of meaning for cinema, for which communication as a heuristics cannot sufficiently account. It further indicates that a new field, and new methodologies, are required instead. With its rigor derived from linguistics, semiotics was a methodology that could supplant the empirical research methods of communication studies. And while film semiotics has not been the dominant approach to the study of film for about a quarter of a century now, the legacy of Metz's shift away from the model of communication has endured. Since Metz first disputed film's status as a medium of communication, all successive and competing paradigms in film theory, from cognitive film theory to Deleuzian and phenomenological and other philosophical approaches, have approached film as an aesthetic object rather than an act of communication.

So why return to the question of film as communication now, as John Mowitt does in this essay?

One answer to this question can be given from a film studies point of view.

It has been argued that film studies emerged as a field of research by defining its object through the triad of canon, index, and *dispositif*—i.e. "cinema" understood as a catalogue of ultimately single-authored masterpieces worthy of hermeneutic effort, created in a technical medium based on photochemical reproduction, put on display in a social situation in which technology contributes to and structures the creation of salient forms of experience and subjectivity. Within the framework of this triad of canon, index, and *dispositif*, Metz's shift ensured that the focus remained on the nexus of technology, aesthetics, and subjectivity, rather than focusing on a purported "bilateral exchange" between producers and audience.

The research hypothesis of "Configurations of Film," a research collective comprised of twelve doctoral students and two postdocs per cohort working closely with a group of fifteen established scholars, is that all three elements of this tripartite definition of cinema—the canon, the index, and the *dispositif*—have been in crisis, or at least undergoing a process of transformation, for some time now. The canon of cinephilia has been vastly expanded, and even exploded, by the emergence of new film industries across the world and particularly by the rise of South and East Asian cinemas and popular film industries in Africa over the last decades. Film in a broader sense is now largely a digital and no longer a photochemical medium, even if the roughly two thousand 35mm cameras still in existence worldwide continue to be used in feature film production.[2] In Africa, the entire output of the various film industries, including the Nigerian English-language production known as "Nollywood," has been on VHS and later digital video for a quarter of a century now. Film distribution has entirely transitioned to digital formats. And the classical *dispositif* of cinema has ceded its primacy to a variety of platforms and contexts in which moving images address and find viewers.

---

2   Personal communication with Ueli Staiger, director of photography, August 1, 2017.

For more than a decade, film theory has been accounting for this tripartite crisis of the canon, the index, and the *dispositif* under the rubric of a "post-cinema" and the "post-cinema condition." Terms such as post-cinema or post-media (Casetti 2011; Krauss 1999) had been extremely productive for thinking about film beyond cinema. However, the case can be made that we have reached a point where the concept of "post-cinema" has exhausted its potential as a heuristic. More specifically, the problem with the term "post-cinema" is twofold. It explains the transformation of cinema in terms of what cinema was, but has ceased to be, or no longer predominately is. It prescribes a sense of "oldness" and "newness" and describes the new in terms of the old. And it makes the crisis permanent, thereby delaying the development of new conceptual tools to account for moving image technologies, practices, and cultures beyond the classical cinema paradigm. Against this backdrop, to speak of configurations of film is a move that is designed to re-open the field of inquiry and move towards new conceptual tools beyond the "post-cinema" framework (De Rosa and Hediger 2017). Rather than reproduce established binaries, "Configurations of Film" is interested in instability as an inherent quality of film, in film's shifting formations, usages, and localizations.

To reopen the question of communication could be seen as part of a heuristic which calls into question all elements of the established definitions of the object "cinema." Classical cinema could plausibly be defined as a form of unidirectional one-to-many communication, i.e. a "mass medium," which was the (implicit) working definition of Holvand, Lumsdaine, and Sheffield. Contemporary moving image practices, on the other hand, include the "phone films" first studied by scholars such as Roger Odin (2011) or the "films poucette," films made with digital devices by children, first studied by Alexandra Schneider and Wanda Strauven (2017), as well as other uses of digital image technology, including short film recordings in video messaging and social networks. The introduction of the smart phone in particular has dramatically reduced the marginal costs of producing a moving image. Film and video have become a substitute for the letter or the message left on a phone answering machine, and apps such as FaceTime have turned video into a medium for "bilateral exchange" after all.

One can of course limit the scope of inquiry to artistic practices alone and remove such uses of moving-image technologies from consideration, or leave their study to communication studies. But this would mean to needlessly curtail film studies' understanding of contemporary moving-image culture. In that sense, a renewed debate about film as communication is not only a welcome, but a necessary item on the research agenda.

John Mowitt's point of the departure in *Tracks from the Crypt* is precisely that "communication is that to which we now have ready access" (24). However, his interest is not to reinsert film within a communication studies framework, nor does he develop a new theory of film as communication based on an analysis of the new modes of moving-image use. That book has been written by Roger Odin. In *The Spaces of Communication*, Odin turns Metz's gesture around and draws on his work on home movies to offer a critique of, and an alternative to, the established "one-to-many" models of mass communication studies from a film studies point of view (2020). By contrast, John Mowitt turns to the cinema in a more classical sense to address the question of communication.

In *Tracks from the Crypt*, Mowitt focuses on "moments in the medium of the cinema where that medium communicates about itself as a medium of communication" (25). If modernist cinema—the cinema of Antonioni, Bergman, or Tarkovsky—dramatizes its characters' inability to communicate, one can indeed argue that cinema also dramatizes, or communicates about, its own ability, and inability, to communicate. How does cinema communicate? How does cinema fail to communicate? How does cinema communicate about communication? These are the three questions Mowitt asks to circumscribe what he proposes to call the "drama of … communication" (42).

To seize the originality of Mowitt's approach, it is important to distinguish the "drama of … communication" from modernist strategies of reflexivity or "mise-en-abyme" (Stam 1992). Drawing on a distinction proposed by linguist Emile Benveniste, film theorists in the 1970s liked to describe mainstream cinema as "histoire," i.e. a type of narrative presentation that strategically erased all traces of enunciation and the basic communicative structure of the film-viewer relationship, as opposed to "discours," a type of presentation that makes this structure explicit (Stam, Burgoyne, and Flitterman-Lewis 1992, 105). On the one hand, the avoidance of direct looks into the camera in classical Hollywood cinema lent credence to the claim that Hollywood films were a case of "histoire." On the other hand, against the backdrop of this binary distinction, any reference to the process of enunciation itself—such as a shot that showed the camera in a mirror, and even the excessive use of mirrors itself—could be construed as a moment of "discours," a moment of reflexivity that liberated the film from the yoke of "histoire." By contrast, Mowitt's "drama of … communication" is both more unobtrusive and more pervasive than moments of reflexivity and temporary transitions from "histoire" to "discours."

Cross-cutting sequences usually serve to create suspense by juxtaposing two simultaneous, but spatially distinct actions, in which the action in one section is designed to thwart the action in the other. The classic example is the train operator riding to the rescue of his distressed romantic interest under siege from robbers in Griffith's pioneering 1911 film *The Lonedale Operator*, a dramatic template which Griffith later infused with racism and reprised in *The Birth of a Nation* (USA 1915), where the Ku Klux Klan rides to the rescue of Lillian Gish's white maiden to save her from being raped by a black man. The cross-cutting template in itself could be read as a dramatization of film's ability to communicate, at least in the sense of creating a communion between separate

14   actions through the mind of the spectator. In *E.T. the Extra-Terrestrial* (USA 1982), one of the biggest hits in Hollywood history, Spielberg takes this figure one step further by dramatizing communication, and more specifically, the mental communion of separate actors, in a cross-cutting sequence. Elliott, the boy who takes the extraterrestrial into his suburban home and develops a special bond with him, goes to school one morning, leaving E.T. behind in his bedroom. While Elliott prepares for a biology lesson, E.T. leaves the room, moves to the kitchen and opens the fridge. He discovers a can of potato salad, which he doesn't like and tosses to the family dog standing next to him. He then discovers a can of beer. As the dog barks, ostensibly to warn him, E.T. downs the contents of the beer can. The film then cuts to Elliott in the classroom, who suddenly and involuntarily burps. Back to E.T., now fully drunk, who walks around the kitchen and hits his head against the cupboards. Cut to Elliott who mimetically feels his pain. As Elliott falls under the table, a blond girl in the background—Elliott's romantic interest—starts to notice that something is wrong. E.T. then turns on the TV and starts to dissemble a toy calculator in order to build a device to get in touch with his extraterrestrial peers. Elliott has now moved to his biology class, where he is about to dissect a frog. Elliott asks the frog: "Say 'hi'. Can you talk? Can you say 'hi'?" Meanwhile, through the communion created by cross-cutting he shares the thoughts and feelings of E.T. as the latter watches TV and works on his communication device. Inspired by one of E.T.'s TV inputs, Elliott decides to set the frogs free and creates havoc in the classroom as the animals start jumping around and out of the window. As E.T. surfs channels, he discovers a dramatic scene of a woman trying to leave a cabin, but who is held back energetically by the male protagonist, who then proceeds to kiss her. Elliott mimetically reenacts this moment in the biology classroom, keeping the blond girl from earlier in the scene from leaving the room and ultimately kissing her, for which he has to step on the back of one of his friends because he is one head shorter than his love interest.

Spielberg's scene has obvious echoes of an earlier famous school
havoc scene, the boarding school rebellion in Jean Vigo's *Zéro de
conduite* (F 1930). But rather than just referencing the Vigo film for
a small cinephile audience, Spielberg dramatizes the way in which
cinema communicates with its own past through television for
all to see. While reprising the modernist concern with communication failure in E.T.'s and Elliott's interaction with the dog and
the frog, the scene is also an exuberant celebration of cinema's
power to create a communion of minds, images, and objects—a
configuration of moving images, and other technologies in a network of communication. As Mowitt argues, we could understand
the shot-reverse-shot pattern as a machine "allow[ing] speech
to take place *even when it doesn't*" (28). Cross-cutting here is a
machine that allows not only speech, but various forms of non-
verbal communication, including mimicry and re-enactment, "to
take place *even when it doesn't.*"

Mowitt's own examples in the following essay are less exuberant,
but they cover a wide range of "audiovisual configurations of
film and video" (23), ranging from *Cool Hand Luke* (D: Stuart
Rosenberg, USA 1967), a key theatrical film of the 1960s, to David
Bowie's "Lazarus" (D: Johan Renck, USA 2016), a recent music
video.

But there is more at stake in Mowitt's return to the question of
film as communication than just an affirmation of cinema's power
to communicate, and a delimitation of that power. What is at
stake here is the matter of communication itself, as configured in
and through cinema. As we already pointed out, for Mowitt, the
starting point is not the impossibility of communication, but an
excess of communication. Communication is something "to which
we now have ready access" (24). This shifts the problem of
communication to a different location. Mowitt quotes Deleuze:

> So it's not a problem of getting people to express themselves
> but of providing little gaps of solitude and silence in which
> they might eventually find something to say.... What we are

> plagued by today isn't any blocking of communication, but
> pointless statements. (Deleuze 1995, 129)

Have we come back, asks Mowitt, to the state that Brecht called "antediluvian" in his theory of radio, "that is, the state in which humans were in possession of a communications apparatus, but had no idea what to communicate?"(24). If so, the question of whether communication is possible is still relevant, but it concerns something different, something that lies beneath the constant stream of communication that we are now ineluctably part of. For Deleuze, "solitude is the condition out of which this missing idea might emanate" (Mowitt, 24), from which we "might eventually find something to say" (Deleuze 1995, 129). Mowitt argues that "Deleuze is, if not mistaken, then certainly optimistic" (24). For Mowitt, rather than solitude, the concept of dialogue is key. As Mowitt writes:

> Crucial in what follows will be an insistence on approaching
> dialogue not primarily as something characters in films have,
> nor as the speaking that human subjects engage in, but as
> an ontological structure, a certain, perhaps onto-theological
> account of the speaking subject cannot do without. (29)

Speaking of an "onto-theological account of the speaking subject" has echoes of Heidegger, and the excess of communication that is not quite communication, or not quite communication yet, may at first glance be read as a reiteration of Heidegger's "Man," the historical, factual background of the subject. The "Man," of course, is a set of conventional, preconditioned views and attitudes, that which speaks the subject, unless the *"Dasein"* manages to seize itself from its state of *"Uneigentlichkeit,"* its state of being in thrall to convention (Heidegger 1996). However, as Mowitt's insistence on the concept of dialogue already announces, it is ultimately not Heidegger who reveals what is in the crypt but Martin Buber. For Mowitt, it is not the solitude of self-empowerment, of *"Eigentlichkeit,"* which offers a way to communication, but an ontological

openness to dialogue, understood as an "ontological structure …
a speaking subject cannot do without" (29).

Metz insisted that film is not communication because there is no bilateral exchange. For all the dialogue that happens on screen, the film will never enter into a dialogue with the viewer. Mowitt argues that it is precisely this non-communication, the lack of a reply, which makes film particularly apt to communicate about communication. In his analysis of the final scene of *Cool Hand Luke*, in which the main character addresses God in a church shortly before he dies, but remains without reply, Mowitt writes:

> Luke is thrown into a dialogue through which something communicates in communication that is *not* communication. But neither is it *simply* the latter's failure. This something is an inhuman or pre-human, thus lifeless operation of the im-personal. The machine in the ghost, … the apparatus of enunciation itself. (32)

In this particular case, the apparatus of enunciation is the technique of film editing, or more specifically, the reverse shot from above to Luke's look upwards in the church that underscores the lack of a reply.

So is film a medium of communication?

With John Mowitt, we could argue that film, particularly in a situation in which communication is "that to which we now have ready access" (24), is the medium which we need to understand what communication is.

References

Casetti, Francesco. 2011. "Back to the Motherland: The Film Theatre in the Post-Medium Age." *Screen* 52 (1): 1–12.

Daney, Serge. 1976. "La remise en scène." *Cahiers du cinema* 268–269: 20–26.

Deleuze, Gilles. 1995. *Negotiations 1972–1990.* Translated by Martin Joughin. New York: Columbia University Press.

De Rosa, Miriam, and Vinzenz Hediger. 2016. "Post-what? Post-when? A Conversation on the 'Posts' of Post-media and Post-cinema." *Cinéma & Cie International Film Studies Journal* 16 (26/27): 9–20.

18 Peters, John Durham. 1999. *Speaking Into the Air: A History of the Idea of Communica-tion.* Chicago: Chicago University Press.

Heidegger, Martin. 1996. *Being and Time.* Translated by Joan Stambaugh. Albany: State University of New York Press.

Hovland, Carl I., Lumsdaine, Arthur B., and Fred D. Sheffield. 2017. *Experiments on Mass Communication.* Princeton: Princeton University Press.

Krauss, Rosalind. 1999. *Voyage on the North Sea: Art in the Age of the Post-Medium Condition.* New York: Thames & Hudson.

Luhmann, Niklas. 1995. *Social Systems.* Translated by John Bednarz, Jr. with Dirk Baecker. Stanford: Stanford University Press.

Metz, Christian. 1974. *Language and Cinema.* Translated by Donna Jean Umiker-Sebeok. The Hague and Paris: Mouton & Co. N.V.

Odin, Roger, ed. 2011. *Il cinema nell'epoca del videofonino.* Bianco e Nero 568. Rome: Carocci editore.

—. 2020. *The Spaces of Communication.* With an Introduction by Vinzenz Hediger. Amsterdam: Amsterdam University Press.

Schneider, Alexandra, and Wanda Strauven. 2017. "Däumlingsfilme: digitale Videos aus Kinderhand." In *Kino und Kindheit: Figur – Perspektive – Regie*, edited by Bettina Henzler, 139–54. Berlin: Bertz + Fischer.

Stam, Robert. 1992. *Reflexivity in Film and Literature: From Don Quixote to Jean-Luc Godard.* New York: Columbia University Press.

Stam, Robert, Burgoyne, Robert, and Sandy Flitterman-Lewis. 1992. *New Vocabu-laries in Film Semiotics: Structuralism, Post-Structuralism, and Beyond.* New York and London: Routledge.

MACHINE

CRYPT

DAVID BOWIE

MEDIATION

FAMA

MARTIN BUBER

JACQUES DERRIDA

COMMUNICATION

TOMBEAU

Tracks from the Crypt

John Mowitt

David Bowie's 2015 *Blackstar* has been understood by critics and fans alike to have a certain valedictory status. For them, perhaps for us, it is a 39-minute and 13-second farewell. A long goodbye. My angle is different. By situating the Bowie/Renck collaboration on "Lazarus" in the context of a meditation on the question once posed by Georg Stanitzek, "Was ist Kommunikation?" I consider the CD and the video as experiments in re-configuration. More specifically, by thinking about the distinctly cinematic iteration of the question of communication (citing here Captain's "what we have here is ... failure to communicate" from *Cool Hand Luke*) I propose that mediated communication embodies the *Ich/Es* modality of dialogue disparaged by Martin Buber. What this invites us to consider is whether "Lazarus" in particular isn't the generation of an audio-visual *tombeau* from which or out of which communication strains are to be heard. Is it "saying" farewell? Is it "saying" anything? By drawing on Jacques Derrida's appropriation of the crypt in the work of Abraham and Torok, I propose that "Lazarus" manages (and the feat is neither small nor insignificant) to communicate nothing. In effect, "Lazarus" is the very sound, not of a failure to communicate, but of a "speaking" emptied of what protects it from mediation. Here, Bowie's gnomic persona assumes a political valence not typically ascribed to it.

My title will likely evoke for some the comic books written and drawn by Bill Gaines and Al Feldstein from 1950 to 1955 under the title, "Tales from the Crypt," and while deliberate, this intertextual gesture calls for clarification. Typically framed in the popular genre of Gothic horror, these comics toyed with our fear of death, but did not exactly concern themselves with the crypt as a locus of communication. The comics were not thinking about *themselves* as communications from the crypt. They were not thinking about what a crypt is, or might be. Here then is where my intertextual gesture breaks off. Specifically, I want to tarry over the crypt, and in particular I want to evoke its connotative density to think about the phenomenon of the *tombeau*, the tomb, whether literary (think Mallarmé and Anatole) or musical (think Ravel and Couperin). More specifically still I want to explore here what the concept of the musical *tombeau* might, as if acting like an induction loop, allow us to "pick up," "receive" from David Bowie's final collection of songs, *Blackstar*. To put the matter succinctly, it is from these tracks that I will engage the problem of communication as a port through which to examine the audio-visual configuration of film and video.

In thus placing the problem of communication in the foreground of these remarks I am in a sense echoing Georg Stanitzek's still resonant question: "Was ist Kommunikation?" a formulation—at once interrogative and declarative—that reminds us that, oddly, in the field of mass communications, we have thought perhaps more carefully about the problem of the masses—do they exist, who are they, what if anything do they think?—than the problem of communication itself. In short, what *is* it, does it happen and how does anyone know? Stanitzek, whose study auto-poetically performed these difficulties, gave—at least to me—fresh import to Gilles Deleuze's earlier observation: "So it's not a problem of getting people to express themselves but of providing little gaps of solitude and silence in which they might eventually find something to say…. What we are plagued by today isn't any blocking of communication, but pointless statements" (1995, 129). Put differently, if communication is that to which we now have ready access, have we returned to the state Brecht—when theorizing radio—called antediluvian, that is, the state in which humans were in possession of a communications apparatus, but had no idea what to communicate? Deleuze seems confident that solitude is the condition out of which this missing idea might emanate. But, I will argue, Deleuze is, if not mistaken, then certainly optimistic. The issue is not formulating, out of a certain solitude, something worthy of communicating, but rather acknowledging that even that most worthy of communication cannot be communicated. Not because we are mediatized subjects (Guattari's characterization), but because communication itself has given up the ghost. Or, stated in the spirit of Kafka's astonishing letter to Milena Jesenská from late 1922: "Writing letters … means exposing oneself to the ghosts who are greedily waiting precisely for that. Written kisses never arrive at their destination; the ghosts drink them up along the way" (1990, 223). In the course of these remarks I will have occasion to return to the figure of Kafka, but to adumbrate with enigmatic brevity, more haunting than the "ghost in the machine" (Gilbert Ryle's famous account of the Cartesian mind) is the machine in the ghost.[1] This machine—in Kafka's letter a means of communication devised at "the moment

1   In the context being woven here it is worth acknowledging that Ryle's formulation was taken up by the Hungarian thinker Arthur Koestler in a text by that very name, and further that "Ghost in the Machine" serves as the title for the fourth album by The Police. Sting has acknowledged and emphasized his borrowing from Koestler, without really thinking about what the mind becomes in the wake of a philosophical repudiation of dualism, or what, in turn, might constitute the post-dualist machine. In a more explicitly musicological vein Larry Kramer in "The Ghost in the Machine" from *Why Classical Music Still Matters* explores how the ghost that is us, literally, plays itself out on the piano keyboard, without ultimately making the twist I am proposing

of crashing"—is what both facilitates and obstructs communication. It compels us to *say* nothing.[2]

Failure to Communicate

Although he never applied it to film, Paul de Man's concept of the "allegory of reading" can be made to serve an important function in the context I am elaborating. Specifically, it helps orient our attention to moments in the medium of the cinema where that medium communicates about itself as a medium of communication. More than instances of reflexivity, such moments act out insights into the way particular films can be shown to pass information to their audiences about their own relation to information. With this in mind I found myself thinking, with Stanitzek's meditation looming on the horizon, about the line from Stuart Rosenberg's *Cool Hand Luke* (USA 1967), "what we got here is … failure to communicate," a line that echoes in the film precisely in being spoken twice, by two different subjects. In its first iteration the line is delivered by "the Captain," who oversees a Florida chain gang that includes among its members one Lucas Jackson, the Luke of the title. It occurs in a sequence that depicts

of thinking the machine (for me, as if translating Kittler's *Aufschreibesystem* literally, the inscription system) as the occasion for its own ghost.

2   Although it is framed as a meditation on the ontological character of philosophy, Giorgio Agamben's "Experimentum Vocis" advances an argument whose resonances with my own deserve mention. Elaborating on Benveniste's well-known distinction between *histoire* and *discours* Agamben, through a commentary on Plato, shows that this distinction is the groundless ground for the distinction between language and being. As he puts it: "Precisely because being gives itself in language, but language remains unsaid in what it says and manifests, being destines itself and unveils itself for speakers in an epochal history" (Agamben 2018, 10). This "unsaid in saying" has its prototype, as a theory of philosophy in Deleuze and Guattari's proposition regarding the plane of immanence, defined in *What is Philosophy?* as: "that which must be thought, but which cannot be thought. It is the nonthought within thought" (1994, 59). In both cases, I am proposing that what is at stake here is what Martin Buber means by the *Ich und Es* dialogue, a dialogue in which (the) nothing is said.

the consequences of Luke's first failed attempt to escape. The relevant dialogue is: Captain, "You gonna get used to wearin' them chains after a while Luke, but you never gonna stop listenin' to them clinkin'. They gonna remind you of what I been sayin' for your own good." Luke (with a trace of his signature grin), "I wish you'd stop bein' so good to me Capt." Captain (viciously striking Luke with a truncheon), "Don't you ever talk that way to me." Luke falls and rolls into the foreground of a shot that has otherwise framed the encounter between the two men from the point of view of the chain gang/audience. Captain, "What we got here is … failure to communicate. Some men you jus' can't reach, so you get what we had here last week, which is the way he wants it. Well, he gets it, and I don't like it any more than you men." The Captain leaves the frame to the left, and we watch Luke stagger up to his knees, the chains conspicuously clinking on the soundtrack.

The second iteration of the line is by Luke himself and it occurs in the last sequence of the film. Having escaped the chain gang yet again and on the run Luke hides in a clapboard church. He enters, notes that the church is empty and begins his concluding monologue:

> Anybody here? Hey Old Man, you home tonight? Can you spare a minute? It's time we had a little talk. I know I'm a pretty evil fellow. I killed people in war, got drunk and chewed up municipal property. I know I ain't got no call to ask much, but even so you gotta admit that you ain't dealt me no cards in a long time. It looks like you got things fixed so I can't never win out. You made me like I am. Inside, outside all them rules and regulations and bosses, and just where am I supposed to fit in? Old man, I gotta tell you I started out pretty strong and fast, but it began to get to me. When does it end? What dya got in mind for me? What do I do now?

Luke, as if anticipating the Old Man's answer, then kneels to pray. A cut-away shot has established that the Captain and the county police are closing in, and almost as if in answer to his Pascalian prayers Dragline (a fellow member of the chain gang and admirer of Luke) enters the church. He tries to convince Luke to surrender, saying that a deal for leniency has been struck. Luke responds by going to a window and, looking out at the assembled law enforcement officers, he repeats the Captain's line, "What we got here is a failure to communicate." A rifle is discharged and Luke falls back into the church mortally wounded. In the subsequent and closing segment, Luke is thrown into the back of a squad car and the Captain directs the officer to take him, not to a nearby hospital, but to the fatally more distant county jail. In the penultimate shot of the film we watch in close-up as the rifleman's mirrored sunglasses are crushed by the squad car.

Adapted from a novel written by Donn Pearce, himself once a member of a chain gang, the film has long been read as the quintessential anti-establishment sixties film. Its Christian, even Kierkegaardian dimension—Luke as a Knight of Faith—has also been emphasized. I, however, wish to make a different point, one that rewords these theological resonances. The echoed line contains Luke's dying words. They fork between the infelicitous epiphanic scene in the church and thus in response to the Old Man's silence, and the Captain, thereby suggesting that Luke is receiving the death *he has asked for*. As Luke's last line it terminates the dialogue between both the law and the church, literalizing Luke's failure to communicate with either. So two summary points. First, it is important to note the difference between the two iterations of the failure. In the first, spoken by the Captain, there is an elliptical suspension of the indefinite article, "a." The Captain says, "what we got here is … failure to communicate," where failure feels grammatically neuter, that is general, rather than *either* definite or indefinite. This makes the Captain's line resonate with an accordingly more "theoretical" tone. When Luke repeats it he says, "What we got here is *a* failure to communicate," in effect stripping the Captain's theoretical proposition of its false generality, and reducing it to the political statement that it is. The change is lethal.

Second–and this will seem rather technical but not therefore irrelevant–in the sequence where Luke has kneeled to pray he is framed in a medium shot and we can see him open his left eye and cast it upwards into the belfry. In a cinematic pattern used to enunciate conversation—the so-called shot reverse—the subsequent shot is a long shot up into the rafters of the belfry, Luke's point of view. Silence. We then return to the prior set-up as Luke says, "Yeah, that's what I thought. I guess I am pretty tough to deal with. A hard case. I guess I gotta find my own way." This is then followed by a very high angle long shot *as if* from the silent Old Man's point of view. More silence. Nothing is said. However, I would argue that this conforms, almost literally, to Jacques Lacan's definition of speech in the "Rome Discourse," to wit, "there is no speech without a response, even if speech meets only with silence, provided it has an auditor" (2006, 206). From such a vantage point even the failure to communicate is a communication, as if to underscore Julia Kristeva's proposition that the human being is a speaking subject. But the question nags: if failed communication is communication, what *is* communication? To appreciate fully what might be at issue here it seems appropriate to note that an important, even decisive, element punctuates the scene, namely, the cinematic *technique* of the shot reverse that effects, even stages, the *effectively failed* communication between Luke and the Old Man. Both it and the nothing said by the Old Man (the auditor) resonate in a silence that, in constituting a response, apparently constitutes speech as speech. Typically, in Western (although not exclusively) cinema this technique facilitates or supports the speech act; here, however, a mode or device of supplementation is brought abruptly forward, a supplementation that stresses the technical mediation that allows speech to take place *even when it doesn't*. In effect, what surfaces in the sequence is the apparatus of enunciation, the assemblage that operates in and through the failed communication. It is the means of this failure.

We Are What It Says

If it makes sense to think of this material allegorically, then the failure to communicate repeats in both the dialogue (the film) *and* the medium (the cinema) and does so in such a way that invites much more careful scrutiny about dialogue, that is, the communicating in the film that transubstantiates the unspoken word of God into the bullet that gives Luke what he asked for. Crucial in what follows will be an insistence on approaching dialogue not primarily as something characters in films have, nor as the speaking that human subjects engage in, but as an ontological structure, a certain, perhaps onto-theological account of the speaking subject cannot do without. Put in the form of a provocation: if dialogue matters in film, if it is worthy of the scholarly attention that has long been devoted to it, this is because dialogue matters to the human animal as such. Such a provocation obliges one, or so I will propose, despite all the attention paid to Mikhail Bakhtin in the waning decades of the preceding century, to turn back to his own "master," namely, the remarkable Jewish thinker of dialogue, Martin Buber. My reading of his work, specifically the powerful *Ich und Du*, will be pointedly perverse, but to appreciate this a bit of summary is required.

Written in 1923, *I and You* (and I will note in passing that I am following Walter Kaufmann's more secular rendering of the German second person pronoun *Du*) is a compact, yet hugely influential formulation of the theology of human existence. Heidegger's *Being and Time*, published only four years later, takes up—however anxiously—many of its themes and references, a fact that eventually brought the two men together at Lake Konstanz in 1957. At the heart of Buber's statement stands his concept of the *Grundworte*, in Smith's translation, the "primary words," words that express the twofold attitude (*Haltung*) of humanity towards and within existence. Defiantly ignoring linguistics, Buber characterizes the primary words as two pairs: I and You and I and It, further complicating things when he insists that "I" is actually an abbreviation (*Abkürzung*) for the phrase, "this man here who is speaking." The entire book then concerns itself with sorting the matter of how these pairs orient and organize human reality. As my passing allusion to linguistics will suggest, the notion that words, especially primary words, articulate relations contains *in nuce* Bakhtin and Valentin Volosinov's repudiation of Saussure's rejection of *parole* as the proper object of linguistic science. Be that as it may, what forms implacably in Buber's statement is an argument that proposes dialogue as the irreducible *medium* of human being. Dialogue is not something we have; it is something we are.

Now, despite the fact that Buber writes: "without *It* (*das Es*) man cannot live, but he who lives with *It* alone is not man" (1958, 52, my emphasis), where the two so-called primary words are insistently entwined, his thought is more typically evoked through the titular formula, "I and You." Relation, as captured in the I/You encounter, is conceived as more ontologically secure than is the separation marked out in the I/It encounter. While a great deal might be said about Buber's struggle to derive the You from the It without triggering the paradox of two first principles, my stress, and I have acknowledged its perversity, will fall instead on what can be said about the dialogue *on or with* the It. As you will have guessed at this point, *this* dialogue is what seems figured in the "failure to communicate" allegorized in *Cool Hand Luke*.[3]

Early in *I and You* Buber, again in a provocative linguistic register, says something important about the It. "The other primary word

---

3   In the "Whistling" chapter of *Sounds: The Ambient Humanities* I have teased out and toyed with the series—sibilant, S, *das Es*—drawing attention to the Freudian treatment of what Strachey rendered as "the Id." While a reiteration of this argument may seem called for here (is Buber thinking of the unconscious, or for that matter precisely *not* thinking of it?), I'll demur. Consider this argument as a constant murmur accompanying these remarks.

is the combination (*Wortpaar*) I-It, wherein, without change in the primary word, one of the words He and She can replace It" (15). Given that "it" is precisely neuter, how can that be? A clue is offered later when, in discussing humanity's relation to God, Buber writes: "Men have always addressed their eternal You with many names. In singing of Him who was thus named they always had the You in mind: the first myths were hymns of praise. Then the names took refuge in the language of It; men were more and more strongly moved to address their eternal You as an It" (99). Clarified here is that naming God "Him" (setting aside Mary Daly's misgivings for the moment) is a fateful step away from the You toward the It. Why? Because He or She, but here Him, can *substitute* for the It. What authorizes Buber's assertion is the grammatical fact, as Emile Benveniste reminded us, that the third person—he, she, it, etc.—*is not a person at all*. It is precisely im-personal. While this might suggest or even imply that It is divine, that is, inhuman, Buber regards it as, in effect, the opposite. In a lovely figure he warns against a theology of "falling upwards," that is, *falling* out of the profane *up* into the sacred. That is, of misrecognizing the fundamental horizontality of paradise. That said, when, anticipating Derrida's encounter with his cat by nearly 80 years, he asks, on behalf of the cat, "Do I [the cat] exist in your sight. . . What is it that comes to me? What is it?" (125), add-ing that, "the 'it' here is to be imagined as the streaming human glance (*strömenden Menschenblick*)," that is, the visual encounter between the human animal and the nonhuman animal from the latter's point of view but *as voiced by the human*. As you will appreciate, this clouds the ontological waters because cat and God are equally im-personal, but in a way that places unbearable strain on the sense of "equal."

What this invites, I will argue, is consideration of the fact that Buber's It is more difficult to parse, to pin down than its routinely dismissive pairing with the You might suggest. Perhaps It is the watchword of separation because it is separated from itself, naming, as has just been established, the *Blick* through which the human animal imagines that the animal engages the very power and range of the dialogic relation. For film scholars, this "glance," as Smith renders it, bears an uncanny resemblance to the "gaze" that frames Luke in his "dialogue" with the Old Man moments before he is killed. Luke speaks both for and to the one who gazes down in silence, and in failing to communicate, Luke is thrown into a dialogue through which something communicates in communication that is *not* communication. But neither is it *simply* the latter's failure. This something is an inhuman or pre-human, thus lifeless operation of the im-personal. The machine in the ghost, or, as put earlier, the apparatus of enunciation itself.

Significantly, I will argue, Buber explores, however gingerly, these resonances of the It by insisting that the eternal You, that god, is "wholly Other" (*ganz Andere*) and this despite his immediate qualification that god is also "wholly Same" (*ganz Selbe*), a formulation that leads to the discreetly Freudian proposition, "he is nearer to me than my I" (104). Weirdly, the figure of, indeed the very name for, relation as such is thus the wholly Other that separates the "my" from the "I." Such observations suggest that, among other things, Buber, despite his obvious sensitivity to grammar, writes down his speech without always tracking how It speaks, as it were, without him.

Be that as it may, given Buber's invocation of the "wholly Other," you will not be surprised to learn that *I and You* attracted the sustained critical attention of Emmanuel Levinas, a theoretical voice much more familiar to our contemporary ears. I invoke him here because Levinas's critique underscores motifs of increasing pertinence as I turn more directly to explore the terms of my title: tracks from the crypt.

Absolutely Cryptic Communication

In 1986 Levinas gave an interview to Anne-Catherine Benchelah. It appeared under the title "The Proximity of the Other," and it gives expression to what Levinas will later call his acute wariness of "the philosophy of dialogue" (2001, 193). Asked whether the other would be alterity itself, Levinas responds:

> Buber says that when I say 'Thou,' I know that I am saying 'Thou' to someone who is an I, and that he says 'Thou' to me. Consequently, in the I-Thou relation, we are from the outset in society with each other, but this is a society in which we are equals, the one in regard to the other; I am to the other what the other is to me. My aim consisted in putting into question this initial reciprocity with the other whom I address. (213)

Put differently, while conceding that "whoever walks on Buber's ground owes allegiance to Buber" (179), Levinas is here agreeing with Benchelah that Buber's "wholly Other" is not wholly other enough, it does not achieve the condition of alterity itself. Because Buber's "other," the eternal You, remains the subject of the I's address, dialogue is not only possible, but for Levinas it is *presupposed* rather than established or grounded. In play/at stake here is the very concept of the human animal as a speaking subject.

It is true that Levinas does not develop the potential tie between the "other as alterity" and the It, but he *does* say the following: "Yet the apparent simplicity of the I-Thou relation in its very asymmetry, is again disturbed by the appearance of the third man who places himself beside the other, the Thou. The third is himself a neighbour, a face, an unreachable alterity" (214). The reference here is not to Carol Reed's brilliant film, but, I suggest, to the third person, that is, the im-personal pronoun, It. To again cite Levinas, "This 'it' marks the impersonal character of this stage in which impersonal consciousness experiences something without objects, without substance—a nothing that is not a nothing, for this nothing is full of murmuring, a murmuring which is unnamed" (212). For Buber, as you will recall, God is what is or ought to be unnamed, and under no circumstances named with the third person pronoun Him behind which lurks the It.

34   For Levinas, what is unnamed, perhaps even unnameable, is
the murmur that fills a no-thing that is not nothing. This sound,
precisely to the extent that it resounds in and as the im-person,
ought to interest us more than it interests Levinas. It will certainly
interest me.

In *Sounds* I developed the distinction between the murmur and
the whisper in some detail, noting the interesting tendency
within French to associate murmuring with non-human sounds,
for example, insects. Although broadly pertinent here, I want
to stress something else. To invoke an earlier turn of phrase,
the murmur might better be said—explicitly in keeping faith
with Levinas's critique of Buber—to designate the sound of the
machine in the ghost, the resonance of an operating that, like
alterity itself (according to Levinas) comes before knowledge.
But—and the question seems obvious enough—does the
machine, and more specifically, the cinema machine really fit
here? It does. Commenting on the one evocation of the cinema
that appears in *I and You*, I think the point can be secured. This
evocation occurs in the final section of Part Two where Buber is
exploring the motif of alienation, that is, the sense that arises
within the I that it is torn asunder by its estrangement from the
world of the It. Under such circumstances the I turns to thought
(*Denken*) as the site of mediation between the I and the world.
Through an elaborate figure whereby thought projects strips of
images—Buber characterizes them as cinematographic (1996,
95)—on opposite sides of a room, each captioned, "One and all,"
Buber decisively renders cognitive mediation mediatic. Since,
in the terms of his parable, one wall contains images of "the
soul" and the other images of "the world," the alienated I tries
to comfort itself by turning from side to side. In effect, panning.
But, and Buber's fascination with the cinematic technique of the
superimposed image is plain, what happens if the walls converge in the flash of an overlap between their respective strips
of images? As he writes: "A deeper shudder seizes him," (96) a
formulation I read as evoking his recognition that precisely to

the extent that thought thinks in images, it can only intensify the alienation it is otherwise called upon to quell. Typically, this sort of formulation is read as delimiting the power of thought in an ontology of dialogue, but it seems to me that it can also be read as an acknowledgement of the radical alterity that murmurs within the im-person, the It. The cinematic image is not here merely an example; it is also a device deployed *within thought* to acknowledge what rattles both its attention and its attunement.

What, in the wake of this, might we say about the machine of phonography, or more broadly, the recording of sound, whether in the form of a murmur or in the form of music? What or where is its ghost within which it rattles? Let us then come to the musical *tombeau*. If one takes Ravel's *Le Tombeau de Couperin* as paradigmatic of the form, what one has is a short composition divided up into 6 parts or movements, each in ways distinctive to its formal function or style (Fugue, Toccata, etc.) commemorating the life of the one entombed.[4] Very plainly, the music marks the site of the tomb from the outside, as if echo-locating the contours of the casket.

4   Someone who would disagree with the emphasis I have placed here on Ravel is Susan McClary; not because she accepts Adorno's dismissal of Ravel as trafficking in "disguise" (she has her own fish to fry with "Teddie"), but because Couperin matters to her thinking about a much earlier *tombeau*, Jean Henry D'Anglebert's *Tombeau de Mr de Chambonnières*. Among her several themes is the question of with what historical assumptions do we listen to or attempt to perform the French baroque canon, but her emphasis on the temporality of absorption (akin to what Deleuze means by "the time-image") speaks very immediately to what I thought I was listening to in Bowie's *tombeau*. As she is a much cleverer musicological inchworm than I, I'll not attempt to replicate the level of her attention in my discussion, but when she describes the sonic structure of the *tombeau* as exhibiting the distinctly Gallic properties of a "hermetically sealed jar," (McClary 2000, sec. 41) this struck an immediate chord. Of course, to hermetically seal something (say, a crypt) means to magically (the term derives from Hermes Trismegistus) prevent liquid from escaping its container. In effect, it allows nothing to pass. But what does this nothing that passes sound like? This is the question that McClary's meditation left me absorbed with.

    Striking here is the sonic peculiarity of music solicited from within a tomb that approaches it from the outside. The "voice" of the tomb is thus both beyond and before the grave. Of interest is not only whether or how this voice communicates, but, as I intimated in my opening, what must communication be if it does? Or, and the provocation to thought verges on the intolerable, what if it does not? This is not the voice of the dead, it is a dead voice, a voice filled with the machine that ghosts it. To play out more systematically what is at issue here, especially as this might bear on the ontology of the dialogue to be found in the dispute between Buber and Levinas, I turn to my titular evocation of the crypt, a concept produced in the work of the psychoanalysts Nicolas Abraham and Maria Torok. It helps, I will propose, grasp the peculiar structure of an exteriorized interiority characteristic of the musical tomb, especially when we think about the tomb as a piece written, perhaps as a valedictory gesture, by someone burying him or herself alive within it.

The crypt opens at the semantic lip where the English word itself forks between code and grave. Taken as synonyms, code and grave cross through one another producing the materialization of a set that is not a member of itself. A terminal incompletion. In their remarkable study, *The Wolf Man's Magic Word*, Abraham and Torok deploy the crypt to analyze one of Freud's most perplexing analysands, Sergei Pankeiev (the "Wolf Man"), pushing at the very bounds of what is readable within psychoanalysis. Indeed, as they astutely observe, there is a remarkable topographic echo between the Wolf Man's cryptonyms (they pointedly opposed these to metonyms) and Freud's struggle, in this case history, to secure his science, not from the usual detractors, but from his innermost circle. As suggestive as such formulations are they do not isolate as effectively as does Derrida what is decisive about the crypt, both as a complication of the tomb and as a locus from which either tales or tracks might emerge.

In the wake of the failed optimism of three straightforward interrogatives, "What is a crypt?" Derrida then elaborates:

Constructing a system of partitions, with their inner and outer surfaces, the cryptic enclave produces a cleft in space, in the assembled system of various places, in the architectonics of the open square within space, itself delimited by a generalized closure, in the *forum*. Within this forum, a place where the free circulation and exchange of objects and speeches can occur, the crypt constructs another more inward forum like a closed rostrum or speaker's box, a safe: sealed and thus internal to itself, a secret interior within the public square, but, by the same token, outside it, external to the interior. Whatever one might write upon them, the crypt's parietal surfaces do not simply separate an inner forum from an outer forum. The inner forum is (a) safe, and outcast outside inside the inside. That is the condition, and the stratagem, of the cryptic enclave's ability to isolate, protect, to shelter from any penetration from anything that can filter in from the outside from outside along with air, light or sounds, along with the eye or the ear, the gesture of the spoken word. ([1986] 2017, xiv)

At one level, this drift toward the figure of the forum (italicized for emphasis in the passage), is another tropological manoeuvre designed to underscore the work of the title of the For-ward/word, "*Fors*" in its contents. But when Derrida later situates the crypt on the cleft between introjection and incorporation, insisting that at stake here is the "appropriation and safekeeping of the other *as other*" (xvii), one realizes that forum, public square and the speeches circulating there all conspire to pitch this discussion of the crypt into the fray between Buber and Levinas with the consequence of posing the unnerving question: is dialogue possible in the face of an It that might be designated a crypt? Can I get from It to You and back?

Of equal interest, although doubtless only in the context I have woven, is Derrida's reference to the speaker's box, a reference by means of which, if paired, however asymmetrically, with Theodor Adorno's physiognomic account of the "radio voice," and the decisive role of the "loudspeaker" in generating it, one can grasp how the crypt and the musical tomb might be made for each other. But to what end, or with what effect? If, as has been noted, the musical tomb is conventionally crafted in the wake of a death, that is, as a commemoration for survivors, one is hard pressed here to harken to the music that might be emerging *from* the musical tomb and wafting into the public square, the forum. The crypt, by safekeeping the other as other, that is by sealing itself hermetically, draws attention to the arrogance of commemoration: the music is for us, not for you. By the same token, if the crypt is cryptic because it walls the inside out, then the sounds that communicate through its parietal surfaces *might actually emanate from within.* These musical strains meant for us are not ours, but its; that is, they approach from a *"fors"* that is, as is said, dead to us. The crypt is not for the dead, it is for that which in-animates the living. In this, I would argue, Mallarmé's collection of ashen words, *A Tomb for Anatole*, predicts the encryption of the tomb, *in general.*[5]

Vital here is the clarification that at stake in the encryption of the tomb is not simply a reversal. The point is not that the music of the tomb comes *before* death, rather than after it. Were this the case my remarks would fall squarely within the paradigm of valediction, music as a farewell or leave-taking (a "self-epitaph" as Tony Visconti has described *Blackstar*), and pose little if any challenge to the notion of communication. With the advent of what Friedrich Kittler calls "phonography," the music of the dead has, in principle, long been in a position to communicate with the living, to survive death. No, if the crypt matters here it is because it draws attention to the cleft in space that falls between

5   In his introduction to Serge Margel's *Le Tombeau du dieu artisan* (tomb of the artisan god), Derrida has commented at length on the structure of the *tombeau.* He brings out the points of contact between Margel and Mallarmé, notably the folding that makes their texts into instances of what they speak. Tomes that are tombs. No reference is made here to the concept/metaphor of the crypt, but the discussion that transpires on pages 9–12 invites such reference repeatedly (see Derrida 2017).

the before and the after of death. Does the sound of music that
happens here communicate, does it, can it, open a dialogue? If so,
what is communicated as sound? What is (the) It?

Here we can no longer defer the encounter with Bowie's *Blackstar*
and, in the spirit of our thematic focus on configurations of film,
Johan Renck's video for the "Lazarus" track.

"Lazarus": All or Nothing

There is much, maybe even too much, to say here, but let me
begin by noting that my remarks will not be fanatical. I leave the
details that fanaticism can add here for others. Nor will I attempt
the sort of writing perfected in Simon Critchley's remarkable little
study of Bowie. Instead, I want to explore in what sense this piece
is precisely a track from a crypt, and what air pressure it thus
brings to bear on the theme of the failure to communicate. Let
me also note that my reading, though not fanatical, is obstinate.[6]
It persists in the face of the following comments made by Johan
Renck in an interview with Justin Joffe. Reporting on a conversation with Bowie about the video, Renck cites Bowie as saying:
"The one thing I think is important is not to go into any second
guessing or analysing what these images mean, because they're
between you and me. People are going to go head over heels to
try to break it down and figure it out across the spectrum and
there's no point in even engaging that." Taken at their words I
can now either simply step away from the keyboard, or stress
that left open is the possibility, perhaps even the invitation, to
formulate a *first guess* about the cleft between the images and
the sounds, a cleft announced in the title that introduces a name

6   Although, one might note, not obstinate enough. Among the several matters
     set aside in this reading is the uncanny resonance between the clapboard
     church where Luke goes to die, and the wardrobe from which "Lazarus"
     emerges and returns. The warp and woof of this resonance, however richly
     tangled, may not, in the end, be any more pertinent than the simple fact that
     a certain meta-commentary on communication echoes insistently within it.

that never sounds in the lyrics themselves. Such, in any case, will be my gambit, and so it comes as no surprise, I read the piece not as saying whatever anybody says it says, but as saying, that is, communicating, precisely nothing. As Bowie reportedly says: it's "*between* you and me."

So off I tumble head over heels. Having directed our attention to the lyrics, it seems urgent to bring the piece within the orbit of our concerns, by noting that the first line, "Look up here, I'm in heaven," a line whose first clause is repeated at the start of the second verse, solicits our *Du*, a "you" later engulfed in the pronoun "everybody," who now knows the "I" who has become a me. Here however, the solicitation to look emerges from the face of one who cannot return the look, the face of the character Renck and Bowie call "Button Eyes," the very persona or mask of *das Es*. The visual communication, the exchange between the "I" and the "everybody," is blinkered, maybe even buttoned down. Just the same, *this* is being said. The sounds reach us and in doing so underscore that the image of one deprived of *our* image likewise reaches us, but figured by absence. The It is in the I and mediating, that is parasitizing, its relation to the You. This is what the video says/shows as if a text message on the cell phone (not, by the way, "mobile") dropped below.

Of course, the line "Everybody knows me now," points to one of Bowie's great themes, namely *fama*, and just as it anticipates the star's obituary, it cuts into the "me" differently. That is, it asks which "me" does everybody know? Am I who everybody knows or am I already and forever dead to you? Whence, I would suggest, the shift from heaven to danger in the second verse, a verse that introduces the figure of "the muse" (a hand that reaches up from below the bed) and is visually enunciated through an extraordinary circular tracking shot that executes literally what, following Buber, we might call a "falling upward." In effect, we are here given the cryptic, gyroscopic template of the entire audio-visual communication. It winds around its unwinding.

Reference to verses here calls attention to the musical material as such. The song contains a short intro, three verses, a break— middle eight—and an outro. It is written in A minor, and set in 4/4 time without, on the drum track, a true backbeat. In the verses, the lyrics are delivered with little melodic fluctuation, *quasi parlando*, and supported by a simple chord pattern, a toggle back and forth from A minor to F. Significantly, because it is performed by Bowie himself, the verses are punctuated with an upward, aggressive movement of power chords: F, G, A, effectively reversing the toggle between A minor and F. Drawing even more "delicious" attention to this gesture upward, is a second, lead guitar part doubled by McCaslin's saxophone line that descends, essentially on the beat, from C to B to G. In this "contrary" motion the "falling upwards" assumes tonal form. The middle eight modulates up a third to C and complicates the chord pattern by introducing a third chord, E flat, inserted before F. The outro, and it is truncated in the video, repeats the pattern of the verses. A few bars following the break, the saxophone bursts into an acrobatic solo, holding a note only to leap two octaves above it and on into racing 16th notes, a solo that literally exhausts itself. Indeed, this is visually choreographed so that the third verse can re-establish the tune's animating groove. The rhythmic bottom is held together around the 4/4 pulse, with the bass line (vaguely summoning The Cure's "Pictures of You") agitating it with steady eighth notes and arpeggioed flourishes within A minor and F. The overall feel is what the late great Chuck Berry once called "modern jazz" played, of course, not too darn fast. Indeed, Bowie sought out Donny McCaslin's jazz quartet for the *Blackstar* sessions.

If such details matter it is because they are not the mere vehicle for the images and lyrics. They are not what entombs the body that matters, they define one of the parietal surfaces of the crypt that, with the piece itself, opens in the form of a wardrobe, a wardrobe (the British prefer wardrobe to closet) from which *everything* leaves and returns. Indeed, the entire piece traces this Ouroboros. As such, this draws a certain keen attention to what I, following a habit of longstanding, call the break. Musically modulating into the relative major of the song's key, and shifting into the past tense—"By the time I got to New York, I was living like a king"—this is also where, in a costume recycled from *Station to Station*, Bowie looks out at us with his "own" eyes. If one considers that the name "Lazarus," suppressed in the lyrics, arises in the image, then the modulation into C (played, I note, on piano *without* the black keys) operates as an un-wrapping (pun intended). Emerging from the wardrobe, Lazarus's wrappings are removed as he returns to life. As if to underscore the shift, the final line of the break, prior to the displacement of the voice by the horn, is "I was looking for your ass," where the antiphonal "look up here," of the first two verses, is reversed from the present imperative to the past declarative, and this as the image flits back and forth between "Button Eyes" and "Bowie." You and I becomes I and you, or at least "your ass," a hip hop formulation that through metonymic compression designates its addressee as someone in danger (either real or feigned).

But there is more to the break than this. During it a figure, vaguely but distinctly "female," who has otherwise merely men-aced the frame, emerges as a tormenting muse, reframing the break as a scene in which the drama of composition, and thus communication, is staged. When, immediately prior to the solo, we see Bowie seated at his writing desk, with pen in hand, the bland overarching theme of creativity sharpens into a variant of the *fama* motif emphasized earlier. Put differently, inspiration is here presented as the mad drive to communicate, but under the sign of expiration, an exhausted loss of breath that the saxo-phone mimics as the writer collapses. If the muse menaces from below it is because she demands that saying happens even when there is nothing (left) to say.

The following verse puts two final details into the mix. It reads: "This way, or no way/You know I'll be free/Just like that bluebird/Ain't that just like me?" The salient details are the figure of the

bluebird and the twisted phrase: "Ain't that just like me?" What
makes them resonate is the stress placed on the demonstrative
pronoun, "that." In the case of the bluebird, "that" operates to
refer us not to any old bluebird, but to *that* bluebird, that is the
one we "all" know, that is, the "bluebird of happiness" treated
at length by Maurice Maeterlinck in his play *The Blue Bird* and,
decisively closer to Bowie's heart, sung about by Judy Garland
in *The Wizard of Oz* (USA 1940).[7] In the case of the phrase, "that"
operates, in conformity with Charles Sanders Peirce's account of
the index, as a demonstrative pronoun that registers a preceding
noun, in this case, the bluebird with whom Bowie shares the one
way passage to freedom. Taken as part of the phrase, "that" puts
it in touch with the preceding phrase, and together they—through
the vernacular contraction "ain't"—pose the rhetorical question:
is this, is *It*, not just like me.

But what is It? What is it that Bowie is just like? At the risk of accel-
erating my offensive tumble, it seems worth nothing that both
in *The Blue Bird* (USA 1940) and in *The Wizard of Oz* the bluebird
serves to effect a turn within happiness, a turn that in Fleming
et al.'s film allows Dorothy to finally realize that "there is no
place like home." This turn explicitly traces a cryptic topography
by establishing that the outside, the locus of freedom and
happiness, is actually always already inside. To be "just like"
that bluebird is thus to be free, but in precisely this cryptic way.
Moreover, if we recall that the octave leap that occurs in the line,
"*somewhere* over the rainbow," is precisely the same leap traced
in "Starman" (indeed, the melodic lines in both songs converge
note for note), the song that announced Bowie's "arrival" in 1972
on Top of the Pops, then we hear in the allusive bluebird a similar

7   In the "dueling" careers of Judy Garland and Shirley Temple it happens that
the latter starred in a film based on the Maeterlinck play called, *The Blue
Bird*. Made in 1940 and directed by Walter Lang, the film, although not a
musical, made it clear that, at least from the standpoint of the composer, Yip
Harburg, the blue bird in question was the one given narrative significance
by Maeterlinck. It is a pastoral thus damaged figure not unlike the "blue
flower" dear to both Novalis and Benjamin.

cryptic folding of the end of a career back onto its beginning. Here, of course, the temptation is strong to read the phrase as a valediction—Bowie, like many before him, sees himself liberated from his mortal coil—but we are urged to hesitate here precisely by the reiterated "just like." This is not me. It is merely just *like* me. In fact, strictly speaking, and listen carefully, "ain't that just like me." Verging on litotic, this formulation both reminds us that we know this man well enough to know what he is *likely* to say, but at the same time, that whatever we know about a man who might fly from earth only to return home, this knowledge is hemmed in by simile, by a *figure* of speech.

My earlier demurral about mimicking Critchley's style should not be taken to mean that I have nothing to say about what he says about *Blackstar*. Indeed, I will bring these remarks to conclusion by engaging him directly and, in the process, clarify what I wish to leave you with regarding the question of communication. In meditating on the significance of Bowie's musical theatre piece (co-written with Enda Walsh), *Lazarus*, Critchley writes the following: "Is Bowie Lazarus? Is this why he chooses to use this final persona in order to say goodbye to us? And in choosing the character of Lazarus as the one who is unable to die is Bowie even saying goodbye?" (2016, 219). After a brief detour through a different Kafka—not the Kafka of the correspondence with Milena but Kafka the author of "The Hunter Gracchus"—he turns to puzzle out his hesitation about the valedictory character of *Blackstar* writing: "They [Gracchus, Lazarus and Newton—Bowie's character in Roeg's *The Man Who Fell to Earth* (UK 1976)] occupy the space between the living and the dead, the realm of purgatorial ghosts and spectres. Perhaps Bowie is telling us that he also occupies that space between life and death, that his art constantly moved between these two realms, these two worlds, while belonging fully to neither" (220). While there is much to agree with here, I hope you will understand why, and on which terms, I think more precision is warranted. "Ghosts and spectres"?

Recall that "Lazarus" appears on the lip of both the video and
the song in their titles. It appears as a word, thus an image, and
precisely a word that is not said, that is silent. Moreover, insofar
as "Lazarus" *appears* inside the work, he appears precisely as a
figure, that is, someone just *like* himself, a figure who emerges
from off-screen space, the wardrobe, to which it later returns.
The sounds from which the word "Lazarus" is absent happen in
the space between the departure and return of this figure to the
wardrobe. Earlier, I proposed that the wardrobe be better taken
as a crypt, but what that implies can now be clarified. If the crypt
is this impossible structure of parietal surfaces across which the
self and the wholly other are distributed, then to associate the
crypt with the wardrobe means that it manifests not in the piece
of furniture, but in the space that delimits what is outside it—
where and when the song occurs—and what is inside it, the off-
screen space of what precisely exceeds both sound and image.
This topography has its analogue in the relation between the
word/name, "Lazarus," and the image/song where he appears,
only and decisively as someone "like" "Lazarus." Thus, if Bowie is
"Lazarus" he is so precisely to the extent that they both are *like*
who they are and are not. They are not only like *each other*, but
they are only *like* themselves.

But let's come to the crux: is he in dialogue with us? Is he saying
goodbye? Is he telling us that he occupies the space between life
and death? What, not to put too fine a point on it, is this musical
crypt communicating? Shifting here to the track from the artist
is important, not because the intentional fallacy would instantly
trigger the fanaticism I have been seeking to avoid, but because
it helps us keep track of the machine in the ghost, the collective
assemblage of enunciation that constitutes the It of any and
every dialogue that transpires between an I and a You. What
becomes audible here is not the word "goodbye," here synony-
mous with aloha, that is hello and goodbye (among many other

things), but nothing.[8] The track from this crypt *says* nothing, but it does so emphatically, that is, it does so by hollowing out the event of communication even as it takes place. In this, let me propose that *Blackstar*—the artwork, the commodity, the file, etc.—is a deeply political gesture, one whose political force can be gauged by recalling what Deleuze was trying to tell us about the contemporary plague, that is, the pointless statements that effortlessly circulate 24/7 through a global communication network that does not block but incites expression. Or, to invoke a quite different although highly relevant point of comparison, consider in what ways *Blackstar*, precisely as a *tombeau,* repeats the gestures of Chris Marker's *Le Tombeau d'Alexandre* (F 1992). Made in 1992 this extraordinary study, perhaps even an homage, to Alexandr Medvedkin executes a carnival of parietal enfoldings—the filmed interview with Medvedkin who emerges as the most unwatched yet influential Soviet director of the 20th century; the narrator's skilful use of the second person to superimpose the audience and the subject; the staging of film viewings within, around, and before the *tombeau* and so on—all cryptic gestures that link the figure of the pure communist (the last Bolshevik) with the effect of a medium that races to say what it marks as unsayable. True, Marker's preferred mask was that of the cat as opposed to "Button Eyes," but his articulation of the tie between formal dysfunction and what we might call primary bolshevism traces a politicization of art that echoes in Bowie's crypt. It is along this threshold, this lip, that *Blackstar* leaves us. As such, its gesture may be even more profound than Deleuze's who, in reverently invoking the little gaps of silence and solitude, appears to be holding out for a dialogue that, even if possible, even if desirable, misses the point, namely that this dialogue is always

8   Since I accept in principle the "failure to communicate," it may seem feckless here to insist that I do not wish to be misunderstood. Just the same, my point above is neither dismissive nor therefore disrespectful. If anything, I am trying to swim against the torrent of often shallow yet distinctly hagiographic praise that has followed in Bowie's wake. And, not to put too fine a point on it: there is more to nothing than nothing. That's all.

only our bluebird, not our blueprint. If *Blackstar* has the immense pathos that it does, it is because in sharing its crypt with us it points ahead to what will have to be very different if we are to pick up what everyone is *not* talking about. This is not God, this is not even a guitar god, this is the world communication dis-order that is happy to facilitate and monitor the endless buzz, especially now the buzz about it-self. Thankfully, on *Blackstar* we have something that overrides this buzz and gestures toward what the nothing we have not yet heard might begin to sound like.

"I can't give everything [whole note rest] away."

I simply wish to thank several people who have kindly shared their reactions to drafts of this text or pointed me in the right directions: Jeanine Ferguson (with whom I first "experienced" Blackstar); Cesare Casarino, Barbara Engh, Carla Farrugia, Qadri Ismail, Kalani Michell, Anaïs Nony and Niloofar Sarlati. Thanks as well to the editorial group for their several astute hints.

References

Abraham, Nicolas, and Maria Torok. 1986. *The Wolf Man's Magic Word*. Translated by Nicholas Rand. Minneapolis: University of Minnesota Press.

Agamben, Giorgio. 2018. *What is Philosophy?* Translated by Lorenzo Chiesa. Palo Alto: Stanford University Press.

Buber, Martin. 1958. *I and Thou*. Translated by Ronald Gregor Smith. Edinburgh: T&T Clark.

—. 1923. *Ich un Du*. Leipzig: Insel Verlag.

Critchley, Simon. 2016. *Bowie*. New York: O R Books.

Deleuze, Gilles. 1995. *Negotiations 1972–1990*. Translated by Martin Joughin. New York: Columbia University Press.

Deleuze, Gilles, and Félix Guattari. 1994. *What is Philosophy?* Translated by Hugh Tomlinson and Graham Burchell. New York: Columbia University Press.

Derrida, Jacques. 2017. *Advances*. Translated by Philippe Lynes. Minneapolis: Univocal Books.

Kafka, Franz. 1990. *Letters to Milena*. Translated by Philip Boehm. New York: Schocken Books.

Kramer, Lawrence. 2007. *Why Classical Music Still Matters*. Berkeley: University of California Press.

Lacan, Jacques. 2006. *Ecrits: The First Complete Edition in English*. Translated by Bruce Fink. New York: W. W. Norton.

Levinas, Emmanuel. 2001. *Is It Righteous To Be? Interviews with Emmanuel Levinas*. Edited by Jill Robbins. Palo Alto: Stanford University Press.

48 McClary, Susan. 2000. "Temporality and Ideology: Qualities of Motion in Seventeenth-Century French Music." *ECHO: a music-centred journal* 2 (2): n.p.

Mowitt, John. 2015. *Sounds: The Ambient Humanities*. Oakland: University of California Press.

Stanitzek, Georg. 1996. "Was ist Kommunikation?" In *Systemtheorie der Literatur*, edited by Jürgen Fohrmann, 21–55. Munich: Fink.